AMERICAN CARS
THROUGH THE DECADES

American Cars
of the
1950s

Craig Cheetham

GARETH STEVENS
GS
PUBLISHING
A Member of the WRC Media Family of Companies

Please visit our web site at: www.garethstevens.com
For a free color catalog describing Gareth Stevens Publishing's
list of high-quality books and multimedia programs,
call 1-800-542-2595 (USA) or 1-800-387-3178 (Canada).
Gareth Stevens Publishing's fax: (414) 332-3567.

Library of Congress Cataloging-in-Publication Data

Cheetham, Craig.
       American cars of the 1950s / Craig Cheetham.
          p. cm. — (American cars through the decades)
       Includes bibliographical references and index.
       ISBN-13: 978-0-8368-7724-3 (lib. bdg.)
       1. Automobiles—United States—History. I. Title.
    TL23.C441   2007
    629.2220973'09045—dc22   2006051056

This North American edition first published in 2007 by
Gareth Stevens Publishing
A Member of the WRC Media Family of Companies
330 West Olive Street, Suite 100
Milwaukee, WI 53212 USA

Produced by Amber Books Ltd., Bradley's Close,
74–77 White Lion Street, London N1 9PF, U.K.

Project Editor: Michael Spilling
Design: Joe Conneally

Gareth Stevens managing editor: Valerie J. Weber
Gareth Stevens editor: Alan Wachtel
Gareth Stevens art direction: Tammy West
Gareth Stevens cover design: Dave Kowalski
Gareth Stevens production: Jessica Yanke and Robert Kraus

Illustrations and photographs copyright International Masters
Publishers AB/Aerospace–Art-Tech

Printed in the United States of America

1 2 3 4 5 6 7 8 9 10 10 09 08 07 06

Table of Contents

Cadillac Series 62

With its big fins, bright colors, and bold body style, the Cadillac Series 62 is a classic 1950s American car.

The roof could be lowered and raised with the push of a button inside the car.

All Series 62s had **automatic transmission**. The driver used a lever next to the steering wheel to put the car into "drive" before stepping on the gas pedal.

This Series 62 was a two-door **convertible**. The Series 62 was also made as a two-door **sedan** and a four-door sedan.

The car's taillights were fitted onto large fins at its back.

The Cadillac Series 62's headlights switched on automatically at dusk.

The Cadillac Series 62 was huge. It was almost as wide as a single-lane road.

1953

Cadillac builds its first Series 62. It was smaller and rounder than the 1959 model, but it had the same engine and power roof.

1959

Cadillac launches the new Series 62s. Its bold styling looked amazing in colors such as lime green and pink.

In the 1950s, the car industry was growing fast. The big car makers launched a new version of a car every year, because people wanted to drive the latest models.

The Series 62 was one of Cadillac's most famous models from the 1950s. It began with a rounded hood and fenders. Over the years, tailfins and more chrome details were added.

cars to be designed by the famous Harley Earl. It is perhaps the fanciest car in the Series 62 line, with the tallest fins and rear lights in the bumper.

UNDER THE SKIN

The Series 62 was very advanced. Its transmission was fully automatic, meaning the driver did not need to change gears while driving.

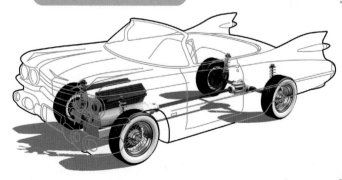

Top of the Line

The Cadillac Series 62 shown here was built in 1959, and it was one of the last

5

Chevrolet Bel Air

The Chevrolet Bel Air was the best-selling sedan of 1957 because it looked good. It was great to drive, too.

The 1957 Chevy Bel Air had a very square trunk. It opened all the way down to the rear fender, which made it easy to load and unload.

In 1955, a small-**block** V-8 engine powered the Chevrolet. Today, many General Motors cars use a larger version of the same engine.

General Motors' chief designer, Harley Earl, gave the Bel Air its angular, modern look.

The owner of this Bel Air painted flames on the side.

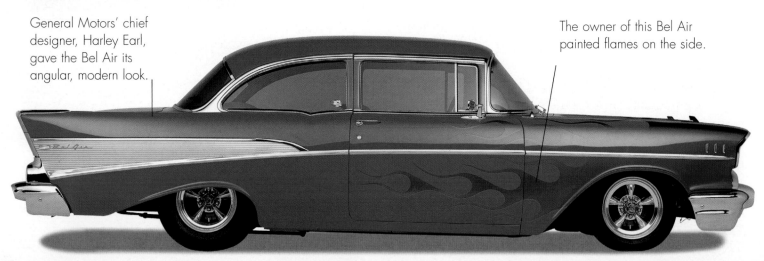

The Bel Air was a common sight across America. It was a family car, but it was also popular with the builders of **hot rods**, who turned it into a racer.

1955

Harley Earl designs the Chevy 150-Series. In late 1956, after a restyle, it became the Bel Air — the famous '57 Chevy.

1957

Chevrolet sells one million '57 Chevys. The car becomes so famous that it is mentioned in songs and appears in movies.

Since the 1920s, Chevrolet and Ford have competed to win the biggest share of the American car market. In 1957, Chevrolet was the clear winner. It sold more than one million sedans and convertibles. The mid-sized Bel Air was one of the best-selling Chevrolets that year. Ford had to wait until 1964 to sell one million of its Mustangs.

All models built in 1957 had a white flash on the side. Later, owners often liked to add their own designs. The small-block V-8 engine and the racing-style wheels were also popular.

Good Value

People liked the Bel Air because it looked stylish. Although it was cheap, it looked as good as some of its expensive rivals.

UNDER THE SKIN

The Chevrolet small-block V-8 is one of the world's most popular engines. It is small but powerful.

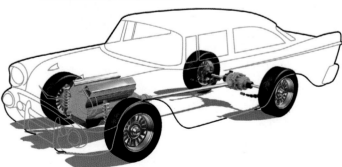

7

Chevrolet Corvette

In the early 1950s, Chevrolet was known for making sensible family cars. Then it changed its image by introducing an exciting sports car — the Corvette.

The Corvette's windshield wrapped around the front of the car, giving the driver protection from the wind.

The first Corvettes had six-**cylinder** engines. Later, they got the famous Chevrolet V-8 engine.

The Corvette's body was made out of **fiberglass**, so it never rusted. The fiberglass also made the car lighter so it could go faster.

The Corvette was small and rounded. Its curvy lines were very different from the big, bold cars usually seen on roads in the United States.

In the 1950s, the car market was competitive. People had many cars to choose from, and Chevrolet's sensible image meant it lost sales among younger people who wanted fast, exciting cars.

Fiberglass Elegance

Chevrolet built the stylish Corvette — a two-seater sports car — especially for young, single men. It was the first mass-produced car made out of fiberglass and also had a very powerful engine.

With its 150-**horsepower** engine, it could easily go faster than 100 miles (161 kilometers) per hour.

Today, the Corvette is one of the most famous models of car — and it all began with the 1950s Corvette.

MILESTONES

1952

General Motors's chief designer Harley Earl shows the company's president, Harlow Curtice, a model of the Corvette. Curtice gives orders to start building it immediately.

1953

The Corvette makes its public debut at the General Motors Motorama Show in Detroit, Michigan. From then on, the Corvette is a huge success.

UNDER THE SKIN

Chevrolet used steel tubes to build a simple frame so that the engine and wheels could be mounted onto the fiberglass body of the car.

9

Chevrolet Impala

The Impala was Chevrolet's most luxurious model, with bold styling and lots of special features.

Even in the 1950s, the Impala had a power roof, air-conditioning, and **cruise control**. It was an advanced car for the time.

Like many cars in the 1950s, the Chevy Impala had huge fins on the rear of the car.

The license plate was attached to the spare wheel cover and was easy to see.

The driver could remove the lower part of the rear panel to change the tires.

The Impala had the biggest trunk of any car at the time. Two people lying side by side could fit in it.

The Impala was designed to ride low. The owner of this Impala has changed it to ride even lower, giving it a fierce look.

1958

Chevrolet first uses the Impala name on an advanced Bel Air model. It becomes very popular.

1959

To build on the previous year's success, "Impala" is used as the name of a whole new model. It, too, is popular.

Chevrolet usually made cars many people could afford. The Impala, however, was more expensive, although not as expensive as a Cadillac.

and used special General Motors **gears**. Later, Chevrolet launched a pickup truck, the El Camino, which was based on the Impala **chassis** and had a similar engine.

Passenger Comfort

The Impala was designed to look long and low. This was a very different and new look at the time. The Impala was also huge, with big tailfins similar to those on a Plymouth or Buick.

Inside, there was seating for up to six people. The V-8 engine was big, at 348 cubic inches (5,703 cubic centimeters),

UNDER THE SKIN

The Impala was the first Chevrolet to use the new big-block V-8 engine. Chevrolet makes Impalas even today.

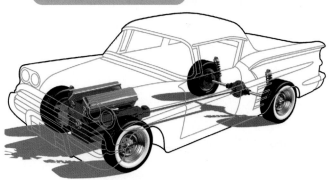

Chevrolet Nomad

The Nomad was a huge step forward for **station wagons**. It was both practical and very stylish.

Chevy V-8 engines powered the early Nomads. Later, some were given even more powerful engines.

The **tailgate** split in two, making it easier to load.

The Nomad's rear window wrapped around the back of the car, giving the driver a very clear view when backing up.

With its rear seats folded down, there was room in the back for plenty of luggage.

Most station wagons have four doors, but the Nomad had only two.

From the front, the Nomad looks like a sedan such as the Chevrolet Bel Air, but from the rear, it looks more like a van.

MILESTONES

1955

The first Nomad appears. It has a stylish hard top and is very practical.

1957

Fewer people are buying the Nomad, so Chevrolet stops selling it. The company concentrates on its sedan models instead.

In three years — 1955, 1956, and 1957 — Chevrolet made three versions of the Nomad. The company gave the Nomad the same front end shape as their standard Chevy sedan.

Built for Salesmen

Most station wagons were four-door family cars. Chevrolet, however, built the Nomad for traveling salesmen. The company decided it did not need rear doors, because salesmen did not use back seats. Its back seats folded down, leaving a flat, clear area that was perfect for carrying a salesman's products.

UNDER THE SKIN

Beneath the exterior, the Nomad was the same as Chevrolet sedans. Some versions, however, had a heavy-duty **suspension** to carry big loads.

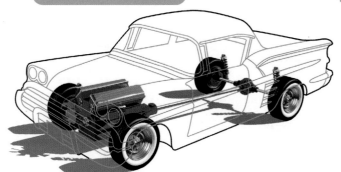

Edsel Citation

Ford launched a new luxury car line in the mid 1950s and called it Edsel. The company hoped that Edsels would be more popular than Cadillacs, but the Edsel was one of the biggest failures ever.

To save money, Ford used the same chassis on Edsels as it used on its Mercury cars.

The Edsel Citation's long radiator **grille** made the car look tall from the front.

The luxury model Edsel Citation had a power-operated roof and a built-in radio.

Early Edsels were not well built. Bits of **trim** used to fall off if the car went over bumpy roads.

The driver could adjust the power seats using buttons on the door frame.

The Edsel Citation was one of the best performers of its time. It could cruise at 70 miles (113 km) per hour.

1954

Ford decides to develop a new type of car to rival the products of General Motors. The Edsel appears four years later.

1960

Ford stops making the Edsel after very poor sales.

Ford wanted to make a car that would appeal to buyers who wanted comfort as well as the looks of a sports car. The result was a new line — Edsel. The new line was named after Henry Ford's son.

Bad Reputation

Many people, however, criticized the new car's styling. Also, the early Edsel models, such as the Citation, were not built well. The Edsel brand came to have a poor reputation, and the damage to its reputation could not be undone. Ford lost a lot of money building the Edsel line. After two years, the company stopped making it.

UNDER THE SKIN

Beneath the bold bodywork, the Edsel was very ordinary. It had a Ford small-block V-8 engine and **rear-wheel drive.**

Ford Fairlane

The Ford Fairlane was one of the roomiest cars of the 1950s. It was wide enough to hold six people — three in the front and three in the back.

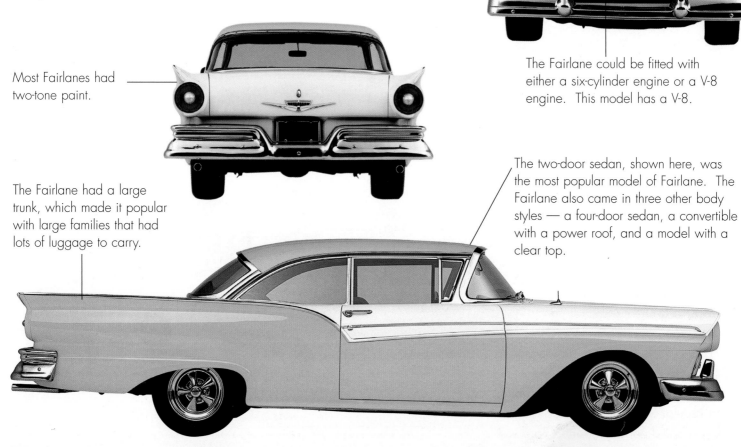

Most Fairlanes had two-tone paint.

The Fairlane could be fitted with either a six-cylinder engine or a V-8 engine. This model has a V-8.

The Fairlane had a large trunk, which made it popular with large families that had lots of luggage to carry.

The two-door sedan, shown here, was the most popular model of Fairlane. The Fairlane also came in three other body styles — a four-door sedan, a convertible with a power roof, and a model with a clear top.

This model has been made into a powerful street racer by putting in a more powerful engine and making it ride lower to the ground.

1957

The Fairlane makes its debut. It is Ford's longest and widest sedan ever.

1959

The Fairlane is redesigned with a new back panel, a low-level radiator grille, and a squarer body.

The Fairlane was one of the biggest cars that Ford ever built. It was almost as big as the Chevrolet Bel Air, its main rival on the road at the time. Six passengers could ride in it in comfort, and it had a huge trunk.

Extra Power
The 1957 model was only made with a six-cylinder engine. Some drivers did not like this because it made the car slow. In 1958, Ford used the V-8 engine from the Thunderbird in the Fairlane. With this engine, the Fairlane was one of Ford's best-selling cars of the 1950s.

UNDER THE SKIN

The Fairlane had a simple layout, with rear-wheel drive, a leaf spring suspension, and drum brakes.

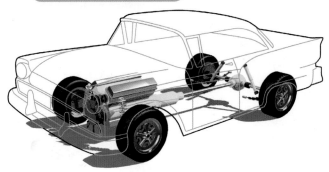

Ford Thunderbird 1955

Ford built the Thunderbird to compete with the Chevrolet Corvette. It was bigger than the Corvette, and some people thought it was more stylish.

The car had a wraparound front windshield, which gave the driver a clear view of the road ahead.

The Thunderbird, like the Corvette, was only a two seater.

Some people said the Thunderbird's mesh front grille looked like chicken wire.

The hood opened forward, away from the cabin, which made it difficult to get at the engine. It did, however, stop the hood from flying open in an accident.

The Thunderbird had small fins.

With a top speed of 165 miles (266 km) per hour, the Thunderbird could go very fast.

1954

The Thunderbird makes its debut at the Detroit Motor Show. It goes on sale the next year.

1958

A second-generation Thunderbird appears. It is much bigger and has four seats.

The Chevrolet Corvette was very popular with younger drivers, so Ford needed to match this by making a sporty, stylish, and powerful car of its own.

Versatile Roof

In 1955, Ford launched the Thunderbird, which quickly got the nickname "T-Bird." Although the Thunderbird was bigger than the Corvette, it performed well and was easy to handle because it was light. Drivers could keep the car's hard top on during the winter and remove it during the warm summer months. The Thunderbird was so successful that Ford still makes a modern version today.

UNDER THE SKIN

The Thunderbird was powered by Ford's popular, small-block V-8 engine.

Ford Thunderbird 1959

Also known as the T-Bird, the 1959 Thunderbird was bigger, brasher, and bolder than the 1955 model.

Twin headlights sat on either side of the car's front end.

Inside, the new Thunderbird had four seats. Drivers who needed only two seats could order a metal cover for the rear bench, making more trunk space.

The mesh grille styling was copied from the earlier model.

The 1959 Thunderbird was a very big car — almost as large as a Chevrolet Impala or Cadillac Series 62.

The 1959 Ford Thunderbird could be equipped with either a normal or a high-powered V-8 engine.

With the roof up, the 1959 T-Bird has a squared-off look that makes it look long and low.

1959

Ford unveils its all-new Thunderbird, which is very different from the first model.

1963

Production ends, and an all-new Thunderbird arrives with an even larger body.

A s the 1950s ended, people's tastes changed. Fewer people were buying the original Thunderbird because they wanted larger, more exciting models.

Built to Cruise

The original Thunderbird was a high-performance sports model, but the new 1959 model was more of a touring car made for comfortable, long-distance journeys. It had a huge trunk and large seats for the whole family.

Thanks to the powerful V-8 engine, it was still a fast car. It was, however, designed for cruising rather than racing. It was luxurious, with a power roof, **power steering**, and electric windows.

UNDER THE SKIN

Like most Ford cars of the time, the 1959 T-Bird had leaf spring suspension and rear-wheel drive.

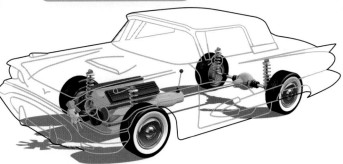

Mercury Montclair

In the early 1950s, the Mercury Montclair was one of curviest-looking cars on the road.

This Montclair has been modified for hot-rod racing. Its roof has been cut down to make the car look lower. Its owner also painted flames on the side to make it look mean on the race track.

The air **vents** on the side of the car were not just for decoration. They also helped to defrost the rear window in cold weather.

The headlights had small hoods over them to keep the light from glaring upward and blinding other drivers.

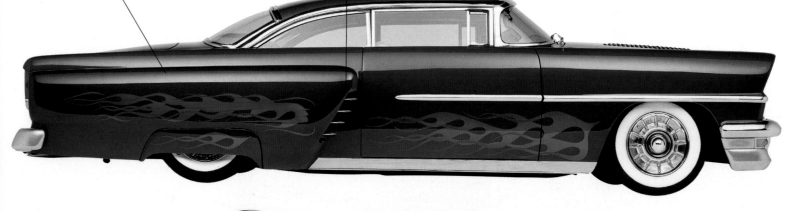

The Montclair had bigger front bumpers than most similar cars, which gave its nose extra protection.

The Montclair had a very large trunk.

The Montclair was long and sleek. It was styled to ride low, making it look like a sportscar, but it was not a fast car.

1954

Mercury launches a new line of models, including the Turnpike, the Cyclone, and the Montclair (pictured below).

1956

The company adds a four-door sedan version of the Montclair to its line.

Mercury is one of Ford's more expensive brands. Mercury cars have always been based on ordinary Ford models.

Luxurious Interior

The Mercury Montclair's styling was unique, but underneath it had the same chassis as the Edsel and Ford sedan models. This made it cheap to build, so Mercury could spend more money on making the inside of the car luxurious.

The Montclair was Mercury's leading coupe model. In later years, its curvy styling made it very popular with people who liked to build hot rods.

UNDER THE SKIN

The Montclair came with an engine called the Y-block. The engine was shaped like the letter Y.

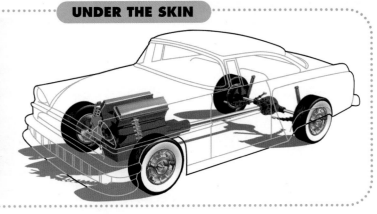

23

Oldsmobile Starfire

The Oldsmobile Starfire was a special-edition car sold in small numbers to people who liked Oldsmobiles.

The Starfire's front end looked very modern for a 1950s-era car.

A 395-cubic-inch (6,473-cc) V-8 engine, known as the Rocket, powered the Starfire.

The Starfire logo became a sign of quality.

The Starfire was available as a convertible (shown here) or as a hardtop **coupe**.

Starfires had power steering, power brakes, and electric windows.

The Starfire's good looks have a very bold appearance on the road.

1954

Oldmobile starts using the name Starfire on its special-edition cars.

1961

Oldsmobile adds a four-light front end to the 1961 Starfire.

The name Starfire was used again in the 1970s on a small Oldsmobile coupe. Most people, however, thought this later car was nowhere near as special as the 1950s model.

The Starfire logo first appeared on a motor-show car in 1953. In 1955, Oldsmobile launched the Starfire model. It was the most luxurious model in the company's line.

The Starfire Rocket Engine

The Starfire used Oldsmobile's famous Rocket V-8 engine, which was fast and gave good gas mileage. Its features included power steering, power brakes, and electric windows. The car was given some new features in 1961, and the model stayed on sale until 1967.

UNDER THE SKIN

The steel chassis and simple suspension made the Starfire cheap and easy to build.

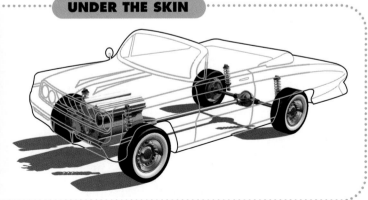

Oldsmobile Super 88

While many car makers were using lots of fins and chrome, Oldsmobile wanted to build a simple car.

Inside, the dashboard looked like a jukebox. It was finished in painted metal with chrome dials and details.

Both the front and rear windows wrapped all the way around, which helped the driver to see clearly at both ends.

The car's chunky front and rear bumpers were good protection in low-speed accidents.

The Super 88 came in two versions: a sedan (shown here) and a four-seater convertible.

The whole wheel was covered with chrome, a shiny metal that sparkled when the car moved.

Oldsmobile made a convertible version of the Super 88.

MILESTONES

1954

Oldsmobile launches its new 88 Series — the biggest cars in its line.

1956

The Super 88 was the best car in the series. It had a larger front grille and more chrome parts on its body than the others.

Oldsmobile's have always been the simplest and most practical of General Motors's many brands. Oldsmobiles were popular among people who wanted a car that drove well but who did not care much how their cars looked.

Rocket Power

Although the Oldsmobile Super 88 had simple styling, it was fast because of its famous V-8 Rocket engine. The engine was more powerful than normal V-8s and could produce 200 horsepower. It could also **accelerate** from 0 to 60 miles (96 km) per hour in just 8.7 seconds — the same as many modern cars.

UNDER THE SKIN

Most Oldsmobile Super 88s had a three-speed automatic transmission. They were also made with a four-speed manual transmission.

27

Plymouth Fury

Most people either love or hate the sharp, bold shape of the Plymouth Fury. It is definitely a car that people notice.

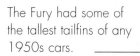

The Fury had some of the tallest tailfins of any 1950s cars.

The grille was as wide as the front of the car, and the front bumper looked like a jagged human mouth. Some people thought this made the car look scary.

The side flash on the Fury only came in gold, although some owners liked to paint it white.

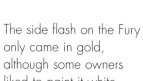

The Fury's whitewall tires were very fashionable in the 1950s.

As well as the gold side flash on the body, this Fury has gold details in the grille.

1955

Plymouth builds the first Fury. Its look is very different from earlier Plymouth cars.

1983

The Fury makes its big-screen debut in the Hollywood movie *Christine*, which is about a scary car that is alive.

When the Fury was first built, there were arguments at the Plymouth company about how to style the vehicle. In the end, Plymouth decided to make the Fury as showy as possible.

Its engine produced up to 315 horsepower, and the car reached a very fast top speed of 122 miles (196 km) per hour.

The 1950s Style

Plymouth made the Fury with big fins and lots of chrome. The Fury was very unusual — its four headlights and big tailfins gave it a frightening look.

Some people thought the car was ugly. Regardless of what people thought of its looks, the Fury was a great performer.

UNDER THE SKIN

The Fury handled very well. Most of its weight was low, giving the car good balance on bends and corners.

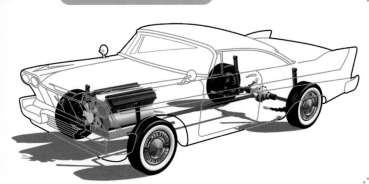

29

Glossary

accelerate to increase speed

automatic transmission a transmission system with gears that change on their own, depending on whether the driver accelerates or not

block the main part of an engine containing the cylinders; the engine block is fitted directly to the chassis

chassis the part of a car body to which the engine, transmission, and suspension are attached

convertible a car with a roof that can be lowered

coupe a two-door car, usually seating two people

cruise control an electronic system that gives an engine the amount of gasoline it needs to keep a car going at a constant speed

cylinder a chamber inside the engine where a piston is forced up and down by burning gasoline to create power

drum brakes brakes that work by pressing against the inside of the wheel to slow the car down

fiberglass a lightweight material made from glass strands and plastic

gears toothed wheels of different sizes that connect to the engine to make it move at different speeds

grille a guard at the front end of the car that lets air into the engine to cool it

horsepower a unit of measure of the power of an engine

hot rods cars that are modified for extra speed and, often, for fancy looks

leaf spring suspension curved sheets of steel used for a car's suspension to give a smooth ride

luxury something special and expensive

power steering a steering system that makes it much easier for the driver to turn the steering wheel

rear-wheel drive a system that sends the car's power from the engine to its rear wheels

sedan a closed automobile with two or four doors and front and rear seats

sports car a car with fast performance and stylish looks

station wagons long cars with extra storage space and windows at the rear in place of a trunk

suspension a system of springs at the base of a car's body that keeps it even on bumpy surfaces

tailgate a door at the rear of a vehicle that can be let down on a hinge or removed

transmission a system in a vehicle that controls its gears, sending power from the engine to the wheels to make them move

trim decorative parts of a car, such as moldings, bumpers, and fenders

V-8 engines that have eight cylinders placed opposite each other in a V-shape

vents slits or openings that take in or let out air or fumes

For More Information

Books

Big Book of Cars. (DK Publishing)

Car. DK Eyewitness (series). Richard Sutton and Elizabeth Baquedano (DK Children)

Racing Cars. Cool Wheels (series). Richard Gunn (Gareth Stevens Publishing)

Corvette. Hot Cars (series). Lee Stacey (Rourke Publishing)

The Story of Chevy Impalas. Classic Cars: An Imagination Library (series). David K. Wright (Gareth Stevens Publishing)

The Story Of The Cadillac Eldorado. Classic Cars: An Imagination Library (series). Jim Mezzanotte (Gareth Stevens Publishing)

Web Sites

Greatest Engineering Achievements of the 20th Century — Automobile
www.greatachievements.org

Museum of Automobile History
www.themuseumofautomobilehistory.com

Rewind the Fifties
www.loti.com/cars.html

Smithsonian Institute — Early Cars: Fact Sheet for Children
www.si.edu/RESOURCE/FAQ/nmah/earlycars.htm

Publishers note to educators and parents:
Our editors have carefully reviewed these Web sites to ensure that they are suitable for children. Many Web sites change frequently, however, and we cannot guarantee that a site's future contents will continue to meet our high standards of quality and educational value. Be advised that children should be closely supervised whenever they access the Internet.

Index